# Saint Patrick

## (385-461)

By
### Rev. Lawrence G. Lovasik, S.V.D.
*Divine Word Missionary*

Nihil Obstat: Daniel V. Flynn, J.C.D., *Censor Librorum*
Imprimatur: ✝ Joseph T. O'Keefe, *Vicar General, Archdiocese of New York*

The Nihil Obstat and Imprimatur are official declarations that a book or pamphlet is free of doctrinal or moral error. No implication is contained therein that those who have granted the Nihil Obstat and Imprimatur agree with the contents, opinions or statements expressed.

# Pagan Kings and Chieftains Rule Ireland

WHEN the Romans conquered Great Britain, they started a colony there and today we find many relics of the Roman days. The most famous is Hadrian's Wall near Closter.

Their winter quarters were in Ireland, which they named Hibernia. Our word hibernate means "to spend the winter," and it comes from the Latin, which means the same thing.

The Romans did not conquer Ireland or set up a colony there. Many regional kings and chieftains ruled Ireland. Druid priests, pagan in their worship and sacrifice, were very powerful. Ireland was an isle of pagan kings and warriors when Patrick arrived.

# Patrick Taken into Slavery

WE are sure that Patrick lived, but we are not sure of the date or place of his birth. The most probable place of birth is Kilpatrick near Dunbarton in Scotland. The most probable date of his birth was between 385 and 389.

Patrick tells us that he was a British citizen of the Roman Empire; the names of his parents usually are given as Calpurnius and Conchessa. His family may have worked for the Roman colony in Great Britain.

We know little of Patrick's early childhood. As a boy of nearly sixteen, he was carried off by raiders and taken to Ireland as a slave. His head was shaved, and he was clothed in a sheepskin tunic and sandals.

# Prayers of a Shepherd

IN his captivity Patrick turned to God. As he took care of sheep, he prayed to God. He tells us:

"The love of God and His fear grew in me more and more, as did the faith, and my soul was roused, so that, in a single day, I have said as many as a hundred prayers and in the nights nearly the same.

"I prayed in the woods and on the mountain, even before dawn. I felt no hurt from the snow or ice or rain."

Patrick's captivity lasted six years, during which time he learned the native language well and also got to know of pagan practices of the Druid priests.

# The Journey to Freedom

PATRICK had a message from God in a dream in which he was told to flee from his master and go to the coast, two hundred miles away. He made the trip safely. He found some sailors who at first refused to take him with them. After a silent prayer to God, they agreed.

After a long journey on the sea, they landed and suffered great hunger. They laughed at Patrick's Christianity and faith in God, but he told them: "Turn in good faith and with all your heart to the Lord my God, to Whom nothing is impossible." A herd of swine appeared that gave them a large food supply.

They continued their journey and reached a settlement. Finally, Patrick was united with his family again. He was now in his early twenties.

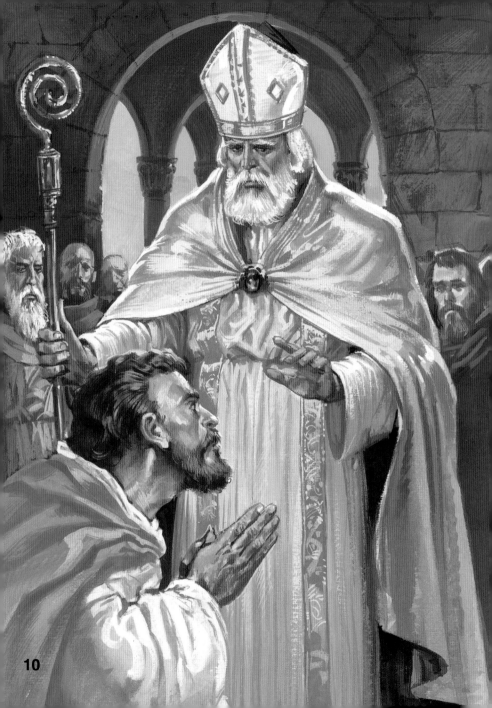

# The Call to Ireland

**P**ATRICK'S peaceful freedom was disturbed by another dream. In his dream he saw the people of Ireland and heard them crying out: "We beg you, holy youth, to come and walk among us once more."

Patrick's heart was willing, but he was not ready. He sought advice and was told to prepare for the priesthood. He started his studies at Lerins, an island near Cannes, France.

He met St. Germanus, the Bishop of Auxerre, and put himself under his direction for learning and holiness. He was ordained a priest and was guided by St. Germanus for many more years.

# Patrick Is Sent to Ireland

POPE St. Celestine sent a certain Palladius to bring the Gospel to Ireland, but he died while working among the Irish. Because of St. Germanus, the Pope told Patrick to get ready to embark for the mission to Ireland. First, he was ordained a bishop.

Patrick landed in the north of Ireland, where he had been a slave. Legend has it that he was met by Dichu, a chieftain, who drew his sword to slay Patrick, but his arm became rigid and he could not move it until he declared himself friendly to Patrick. He asked for instructions and was converted to the Christian Faith. He donated a large barn that later became a church and a monastery.

Patrick arrived at the hill of Slane on March 25, 433.

# Patrick Begins His Preaching

**P**ATRICK soon met pagan priests. Legend tells us that the chief of these priests was able to raise himself high in the air by some magical power; but, when Patrick prayed, he fell to the ground and was killed.

There surely were miracles so that the High King Loaghaire allowed Patrick to preach Christianity throughout all Ireland. While the High King did not accept Christianity, many of his court did.

Also at Tara, the tradition started that Patrick used the shamrock to explain the Trinity. To our day, the shamrock has been the symbol of Ireland, a Catholic nation. At this time Patrick was about forty-five years old.

But there were many chieftains and Druids who tried to harm Patrick. One time Patrick was almost killed by a spear while he was traveling in a chariot.

# Many People Are Converted

PATRICK'S preaching reached the hearts of the people, and he made progress in spreading the faith. We hear of him preaching at Killala with all the people of the area present. The King, his six sons, and twelve thousand accepted the faith.

He was also able to convert the two daughters of the High King Loaghaire.

Patrick went north again to Ulster, and there the chieftain named Daire allowed him to choose any site for a church. Patrick selected a hill in Armagh, upon which he built a church. It is said that the present cathedral of Armagh is built on that same hill.

In the district of Costello in County Mayo, he instructed Chief Ernasc and his son Loarn. A church was built there, where later Loarn was in charge.

17

# Patrick's Sufferings

PATRICK suffered many trials in his missionary work, but he carried on. He tells us that he and his companions were captured and chained twelve times and one time sentenced to death. But, by the power of God, he was able to overcome, and the message of Christianity spread.

A certain prince named Corotick plundered the country where Patrick had been conferring the Sacrament of Confirmation. He killed many on Easter. The next day Patrick sent him a letter begging him to bring back the Christian captives.

Patrick said that he was the Bishop of Ireland and that he expelled Corotick from the Church and from Jesus Christ, Whose place Patrick held, until the prince would do penance and free the captives.

This letter expresses Patrick's most tender love for his flock and his grief for those who had been slain.

# Patrick's Piety

BEHIND Patrick's zeal as an apostle was a deep piety. Many times during the day he armed himself with the Sign of the Cross. He wore a rough hair shirt and slept on a rock. He refused precious gifts that were offered to him. His only desire was to bring souls to Christ.

Prayer was Patrick's weapon. He would often go to a distant place to speak with God. One of the best-known places where he spent forty days and nights in prayer and fasting and where he received a wonderful vision from God is Croagh Patrick, or "St. Patrick's mountain."

Patrick always gave until he had no more to give, and he was happy to see himself poor with Jesus Christ. He knew that poverty and suffering and prayer would bring souls to God.

22

# Patrick Worked Miracles

BY this time, Patrick had many followers. One of the first was Benignus, who was the son of a chieftain and who became his successor. Others were St. Auxilius, St. Iserninus, and St. Fiacc, the son of Chief Brehom. These zealous priests brought the life and doctrine of Christ to all.

Besides the preaching of Patrick and his disciples, there were many miracles: the dead were raised, the sick were healed, the lame were cured, and many wells to this day named after Patrick claim a miraculous flow of water.

Patrick traveled all over Ireland, staying in a place long enough to begin the faith and then he would move on.

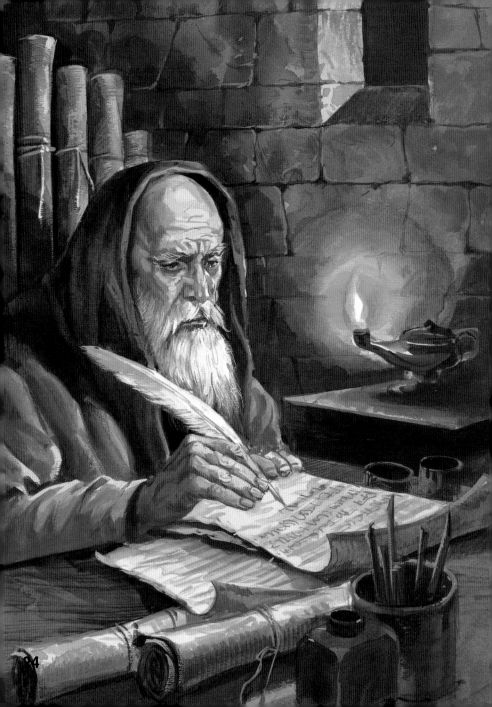

# Patrick's Humility

ONE of the keys to Patrick's holiness is his deep humility. He wrote a book called the *Confessions,* in which he speaks about his sinfulness. He writes: "I, Patrick, the sinner, am the most ignorant and the least of the faithful. . . . I was like a stone lying in mud; and He That is mighty lifted me up."

When he was old, Patrick wrote his *Confessions* as a proof of his mission. It expresses a great desire of martyrdom. He confesses all his faults with sincere humility and praises the mercy of God shown him in his sinfulness.

He writes that he desires to see again his own country and to visit his friends, but he will not leave his people.

He tells us that he himself and all his companions had been beaten and put into prison because he had baptized the son of a certain king against the will of his father, but they were released after fourteen days.

# Patrick's Trust in God

IN his *Confessions* Patrick says:

"I give unceasing thanks to my God, Who kept me faithful in the day of my testing. Today I can offer Him sacrifice with confidence, giving myself as a living victim to Christ, my Lord, Who kept me safe through all my trials.

"You did it so that, whatever happened to me, I might accept good and evil equally, always giving thanks to God.

"God showed me how to have faith in Him forever, as One Who is never to be doubted. He answered my prayer in such a way that, ignorant though I am, I might be bold enough to take up so holy and so wonderful a task, and imitate in some way those whom the Lord had so long ago foretold as heralds of his Gospel."

# Patrick's Success

PATRICK says he lived in constant danger and expected martyrdom, but he feared nothing because he put himself into the arms of God with great confidence.

Before his death Patrick wrote:

"It happened in Ireland that those who never had a knowledge of God, but until now always worshiped idols and things impure, have now been made a people of the Lord, and are called children of God; that the sons and daughters of the kings of the Irish are seen to be monks and virgins of Christ."

By the time Patrick was seventy, it could be said that all Ireland was Catholic and the Church was firm, supported by bishops, priests, and the churches. Never has heresy tainted the Irish Church.

# Patrick's Death

**P**ATRICK continued his missions over all the provinces of Ireland for forty years.

Worn out by heavy labors, he was given the Last Rites of the Church by St. Tassach. He died at Saul, the place where he had built his first church, on March 17, 461.

Legend has it that Patrick's body was found in a church of his name in 1185.

Irish missionaries have brought Christ to the far corners of the earth. They founded the Church in Australia and New Zealand, and strengthened it in England and the United States.

St. Patrick is the Patron Saint of Ireland and the Irish. His feast is celebrated on March 17.

# Prayer of the Church
# to St. Patrick

GOD our Father,
You sent St. Patrick
to preach Your glory to the people of Ireland.

By the help of his prayers,
may all Christians proclaim Your love to all
    people.

Grant this through our Lord Jesus Christ,
    Your Son,
Who lives and reigns with You
    and the Holy Spirit,
one God, forever and ever. Amen.